BRAIN GAMES®

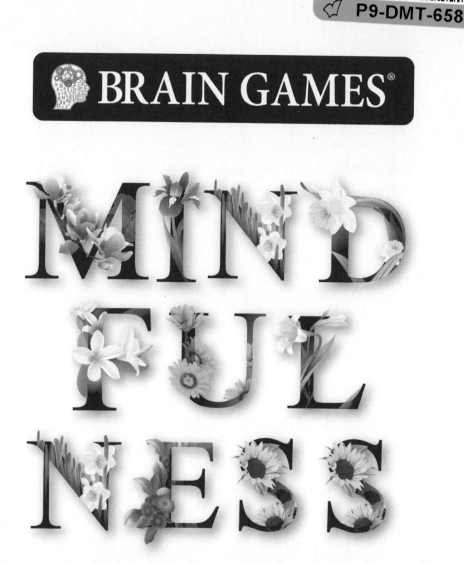

MIND FUL NESS

CROSSWORDS

Publications International, Ltd.

INTRODUCTION

Are you ready to relax and unwind? Decompress with *Brain Games®: Mindfulness Crossword*. These crossword puzzles are perfect for taking your mind off your daily worries, while simultaneously giving your brain a workout. Keep this book in your bag or purse and pull it out when you want to reset.

This book contains more than 80 crossword puzzles with themes to suit all interests and areas of expertise such as foods, common sayings, American history, movies, and entertainment. These puzzles are perfect for keeping your brain happily engaged while helping you disconnect from the stressors of your everyday life.

These puzzles can be done anytime, anywhere. So if you want a quick, enjoyable break while you're stuck at the airport, stopping for a coffee, or waiting in line, pull out *Brain Games®: Mindfulness Crossword* and get started!

TIME AND MAGIC

ACROSS

1. Yellow "Sesame Street" character
5. Golf-course hazards
8. Hanker after, with "for"
9. The Alligator State
10. Like latebreaking news
11. Contributes, as to a pool
12. Took a break
15. Magician's talent
18. Like a seraph
19. Marriage, e.g.
20. Button on a DVD player
21. Run faster than

DOWN

1. "Jambalaya" territory
2. Frightful
3. Quick as a wink
4. Disagree
5. Guava or papaya
6. "Farewell, Francois!"
7. Sushi wrap
11. Forster's "A ___ to India"
13. Athlete's lasting power
14. Exterior masonry finish
16. American symbol
17. "Divine Comedy" author

Answers on page 172.

SCIENCE AND NATURE

ACROSS

1. Sauerkraut, essentially
3. Balancing device
6. Exactly alike
8. Benches and chairs
10. Wall-to-wall coverage
11. Spiderlike bug
13. Like C work
15. Airline seat choice
17. Being
18. Classroom furniture
19. Meet, as expectations

DOWN

1. Casino stack
2. Reference-book sets
3. Alternative to fossil fuels
4. Go-getters
5. Alibis
7. Palate pleasing
9. They end with a zip code
11. Pricey gem
12. Civil War general who became President
14. Locales
16. All possible

Answers on page 172.

OSTEOLOGY

ACROSS

1. A couple of smackers?
3. Elsa's story
9. Letter writing, it's said
10. Little marketgoer of rhyme
11. 1968 film featuring a murderous cheerleader
13. First appearances
15. "Life of Pi" director
17. It might be found at a dig
20. Africa's largest capital city
21. Thing to vanish into
22. "Relax, don't fret"
23. "The Dock of the Bay" singer Redding

DOWN

1. Pond floaters
2. Band chasing bandits
4. Prerecorded, in a way
5. Bodybuilder's motto
6. Ann or Andy, e.g.
7. "A Day Without Rain" singer
8. Downright wicked
12. Dancer's garb
14. Displeased spectator's cry
16. Curly chips
18. Precise
19. "The Lion King" meanie

Answers on page 172.

JOBS AND INDUSTRIES

ACROSS

1. Martha or Rod
5. First Greek letter
8. Detectives
9. "... silk purse out of a sow's ___"
10. They're equal and opposite
12. "___ Gets Drafted" (1942 Disney cartoon)
13. "Duck!" and "Timber!"
15. "Great" Macedonian king
16. Balloon-breaking sound
18. Hollywood's business
20. "Days of Our Lives" setting
21. Sheaths, shifts, jumpers

DOWN

1. "Chattanooga Shoe ___ Boy"
2. Ecological
3. Land of the wallaby
4. "Made in ___"
5. "___ approved" (hotel sign)
6. Focus group?
7. "A" on box scores
11. Freedom from bigotry
12. Some casino staff
14. "Early Sunday Morning" artist Hopper
17. Deer trails, maybe
19. Truck make

Answers on page 172.

MISCELLANY

ACROSS

1. QB's toss
3. Phone playback
9. Red-carpet greeting
10. Follow as a result
11. Magazine highlight
13. Casual shoe
14. Catnap
16. "What a surprise!"
19. Monastery head
21. Coal bucket
22. One of the red wines
23. Farm sight

DOWN

1. Slapstick antic
2. "Kinda" kin
4. Less demanding
5. Like some Chinese food
6. Nitrogen or neon
7. "The Call of the Wild" transport
8. Ice spinner
12. Not honor, as a promise
15. Virtuous
17. Actor in a crowd scene
18. After-bath powder
20. Seafood shack handout

13

Answers on page 173.

A GLITZY LIFESTYLE

ACROSS

1. Down the quarterback
3. Light and filmy
9. Curly lock
10. Clamor
11. Luxury in some homes
13. Sheriffs and marshals
15. French eatery
17. Deep sorrow or anguish
19. Big payoff game
20. Cocktail for 007
21. Euclid's subject
22. Go steady with

DOWN

1. Fall behind
2. Craft for Hiawatha
4. One-up with smarts
5. PR agents, often
6. Nickname for a handy guy
7. Asian food staple
8. Dapper Dan
12. Precipitous plunge
14. "Good job!"
16. Mallet
18. "The Good Earth" locale
19. Huey or Howie

Answers on page 173.

PHRASES FOR A ROAD TRIP

ACROSS

1. Many emojis
5. A bit off
8. Gets by with less
9. Cairo's country
10. Cornucopia
12. Couch potato's gadget
14. Black eye, slangily
16. Spider or worm
19. Bullwinkle's flying squirrel friend
20. Repeat
21. Tiger of golf
22. Capitol highlight

DOWN

1. "Ditto"
2. Comic-book aide
3. Lovely to look at
4. Charlie Brown's beagle
5. Whine from the backseat
6. Superman's birthplace
7. Steam-engine pioneer
11. It's not clearly defined
13. Casablanca's country
15. "Yes, cap'n!"
17. Like a braid
18. Challenge to a gunslinger

Answers on page 173.

STORIES AND SAYINGS

ACROSS

1. Sanctuaries
5. "Kaboom!"
8. Atlanta's Omni e.g.
9. Watches someone else's kitties, perhaps
10. Inspirational tale
11. Jam or pickle
12. Dish the dirt
15. "Holy cow!", to Annie
19. Easily stretched
20. Dens
21. Crawl or swarm
22. "Maltese Falcon" writer

DOWN

1. Flag support
2. Shades, e.g.
3. Country singer's quality
4. Jurassic Park critter
6. Baja buddy
7. Dress in one's Sunday best
11. Notably significant
13. Conjecture
14. O'Hara's "My Friend ___"
16. Colorful playing marble
17. Nothing, slangily
18. Fiber used in rug-making

Answers on page 173.

GRAB BAG

ACROSS

1. Doesn't hog
7. Pantomimed parlor game
8. Hardly a quick walk
9. Rude
10. Hardly fitting
12. Fist pump or high-five, e.g.
14. San Francisco's region
16. Big map book
20. Rock-star wannabes
21. Bottom line
22. Small biters
23. Cantankerous

DOWN

1. Big-game expedition
2. Site of many a 1-Down
3. Lady's son, in a Disney film
4. Stroll leisurely
5. Ore-Ida morsel
6. Streaker in the sky
11. Site of swings and a sandbox
13. Tense
15. Online retail giant
17. Female TV dog played by males
18. Revealing, as a bikini
19. Calf-roping rope

Answers on page 174.

EVOCATIVE PHRASES

ACROSS

1. Gives a little leeway
8. Ballpark nibbles
9. "Snowy" marsh bird
10. Auto gear
11. Bird that lays the largest eggs
12. Carroll's "Mad" tea drinker
13. Server on skates, in the '60s
16. Christmas-pageant trio
18. Accumulate, as wealth
20. Olympic speed skater Ohno
21. Hard to pin down
22. Feeling before entering a haunted house, maybe

DOWN

1. Arrow-shooting cherub
2. Hopper in depression? No, a British sausage dish
3. Sleep, informally
4. Army mule, for one
5. Bloodhound's clue
6. It might help keep you out of jail
7. Whopper topper
12. Relaxing soak
14. Generally speaking
15. Nightclub or bar mitzvah feature
17. Garlicky mayo
19. Crockpot dishes

Answers on page 174.

VIVID PHRASES

ACROSS

1. Best seat in the house, often
2. Almond-flavored liqueur
8. Look over closely
9. Bar brew
10. Court invitation
12. Like a garden aroma
14. Capital of Kansas
17. Mr. T catchphrase
20. Labor group
21. Indicated a direction
22. Big source of omega-3 fatty acids
23. Castle stronghold

DOWN

1. When depressed, it creates capitals
3. "The Wind in the Willows" croaker
4. Healthy, as a complexion
5. Intern, for instance
6. "Beetle Bailey" bulldog
7. "___ the thought!"
11. Phoned
13. Copy in a museum
15. Pushkin's "Eugene ___"
16. Bread or milk, e.g.
18. Salad servers
19. Magic dragon of song

Answers on page 174.

MONEY AND MOUNT OLYMPUS

ACROSS

1. Old West lawman
4. Like bubble baths
7. Longing for "the good old days"
8. Arc de Triomphe city
10. Bridge framework
11. Tightwads
13. Like "gloom" and "doom"
15. Caravan pit stop
17. Request to one on a sofa
18. Bus rider's "coin"
19. Like a sound argument

DOWN

1. Show some backbone, slangily
2. It's usually inadmissible
3. Zeus's weapon
4. Polished and urbane
5. Pays attention to detail
6. Mainers, for instance
9. Small-time
11. Continue steadfastly
12. Salad morsel
14. "Let's do this!"
16. Begin a tennis game

Answers on page 174.

OXYMORONS

ACROSS

3. They feuded with the McCoys
7. Annual book of facts
8. Bricks that snap together
9. With 10-Across, "big-little" oxymoron
10. See 9-Across
12. Sly and inventive
14. Lake ____ (source of the Mississippi)
16. With 18-Across, "unarranged arrangement" oxymoron
18. See 16-Across
21. Civil wrongs
22. Messed up
23. Hoodwink

DOWN

1. Pancake
2. Peg Bundy or Marge Simpson
3. Place to loiter with pals
4. Hammock occupant
5. Peas, beans, etc.
6. Backtalk
11. Newfoundland neighbor
13. "Ocean," to "canoe"
15. Defeat easily
17. Mirror-ball dance genre
19. Barbie and Raggedy Ann
20. Ticket leftover

Answers on page 175.

PREDICTIONS AND FORECASTS

ACROSS

1. Frisky, like puppies
5. Permit
8. Daisy-plucking words
9. Any pro sports team, e.g.
11. Curly, Moe or Larry
12. Hundred-buck bills
14. Kirk Douglas gladiator role
16. Warren Buffett's nickname
17. Barely-there underwear
18. Nonsense

DOWN

1. Linguine or rigatoni
2. John Hersey story about a small Italian town in WWII
3. Cafeteria brawl
4. Elbow room
6. Metaphorical limit (or desert dare)
7. 1985 Harrison Ford film set in Amish country
10. Covered wagon
11. Size up or solve, in British slang
13. Pantomime, or misbehave
15. Cutting edge

Answers on page 175.

PLACES AND EVENTS

ACROSS

1. Construction area marker
3. Like some easy-open bottles
8. Miser McDuck
9. 1979 Sigourney Weaver thriller
10. Fountain reward of myth
13. Wine popularized by "Sideways"
14. Whistle-stop
17. Top story
18. Shea team, familiarly
19. Pedigreed animal
20. Bigmouth, e.g.

DOWN

1. Toiletry that beautifies
2. Clara Barton, e.g.
4. First game of the year
5. Game played on a plastic mat
6. Window section
7. Barbecue veggie eaten with one's hands
11. "See ya!"
12. Nadia and Olga, e.g.
13. Joker who often elicits groans
15. End of the Greek alphabet
16. Like a wrung washcloth

Answers on page 175.

COMMON PHRASES

ACROSS

5. Receive a promotion
7. Was able to endure
8. Dorm room light
9. Midnight fridge visit
10. How destitute people may live
12. Calling the shots
14. Basic teachings
15. Water conduit
17. Be cruel to
18. 1994 Johnny Depp title role

DOWN

1. Jacob's eleventh son
2. Watered down
3. Circumvent
4. Come to an end
6. Obey the rules
7. Tailor's tool
11. Absolutely no one
12. Economical way to buy
13. Account for holding
16. Break of day

Answers on page 175.

MELANGE

ACROSS

1. Vatican sentinel
7. Andean wool source
8. Feels at home
10. Elongated key
11. Home of Baylor University
13. Admission of guilt
15. Big game caravan
17. Gently urge
18. Polite prevarication
21. Be dressed in
22. ____ Domingo
23. Behave yourself

DOWN

1. Car dealer's spiel, e.g.
2. Ivanka's mom
3. Place of turmoil
4. Old Glory, briefly
5. Big cracker brand
6. Noisy summer bug
9. House trailer
12. Tacky quality
14. After a fashion
16. "What's there to lose?"
19. Hawaiian island or a veranda
20. Cancun coin

Answers on page 176.

HODGEPODGE

ACROSS

5. Cause of odd weather
7. Bound by routine
9. "Jeopardy!" emcee, e.g.
10. The nitty-gritty
14. Amazing to behold
16. Supposed face in the sky
19. For nothing
20. Catch fire

DOWN

1. Very thin layer
2 John of "Dynasty"
3. "Flintstones" pet
4. Floats ashore
6. Brewpub beverages
8. Bear among the stars
11. Nicollette of "Desperate Housewives"
12. Tailor's objective
13. Loosen, as a lace
15. Agricultural building
17. Panzer division vehicle
18. "You gotta be kidding!"

Answers on page 176.

CHARACTERS AND PHRASES

ACROSS

1. Rustic film couple of "The Egg and I"
7. Workaday grind
8. Border collie's flock
9. "Humble" home
10. Trees favored by giraffes
11. Birds often made in origami
13. Desert succulent
16. Impressive and then some
17. Fiery gemstones
20. Former Swedish imports
21. Beach near Diamond Head
22. Be kept waiting

DOWN

1. "The Sound of Music" lady
2. Animated canine or Houston ballplayer
3. Sharpshooter
4. Moniker for Tarzan
5. "Cats" poet
6. Brings to light
11. Great work of literature
12. In days of yore
14. Eradicate
15. Baseball great Reese
18. Licorice-flavored herb
19. Clipper features

Answers on page 176.

COMPETITION AND CONFLICT

ACROSS

1. Commonplace
4. Clique members
6. Alabama, on the field
7. After-workout woes
9. Attack physically
11. Down Under dweller
13. Revived
16. Marrakesh marketplace
18. Cops' patrol areas
20. Historic but fatal Greek gift
21. Chopping tool
22. Cream puffs' cousins

DOWN

1. Prepare for camp, say
2. Dance with high kicks
3. Fake name
4. Like Napoleon on Elba
5. In no danger
8. Curvy letter
10. Braggarts
12. Space Needle city
14. "Simpsons" tavern owner
15. Decorative
17. Brick in the Southwest
19. Big cheese in Greece

Answers on page 176.

AVOIDANCE TACTICS

ACROSS

1. Liberate
4. About 30% of the Earth's land
8. Language in which "simba" means "lion"
9. Cry crocodile tears on stage
10. Rorschach image
12. Avoid commitment
15. "Moby Dick" narrator
18. Eliot's "The ___ Land"
19. "Hips Don't Lie" singer
20. Chief Norse god
21. Like Fosdick

DOWN

1. Most cheeky
2. Express gratitude
3. Avoid taking a stand
5. Football formation (or kind of wedding?)
6. "I'm with you!"
7. Ism
11. WWII fighter planes
13. Big name in hot sauce
14. Yankee Doodle Dandy, to Uncle Sam
16. Japanese cartoon art
17. Specialized police squad

Answers on page 177.

FOOD AND SLEEP

ACROSS

1. They may raise some people's spirits
5. Lifeguard's beat
8. "Au revoir!" relative
9. Ripens
10. Get a midnight snack, say
11. Salad bar stuff
12. Frost's field
15. Jabbers
18. Figure on a box of Wheaties
19. Carroll girl
20. Aunt Jemima product
21. Movie house

DOWN

1. Flight that never takes off
2. Dopey
3. Insomniac's trick
4. Cook just below boiling
5. It shows your gains and losses
6. Biting to the taste
7. Nylons, fishnets, etc.
11. Belly laughs
13. One who's going places
14. Cricket, e.g.
16. Dislike and then some
17. Asparagus stalk

Answers on page 177.

DOUBLE VISION

1. "That sounds about right"
4. Black-tie blowout
8. Talk radio source, often
9. Hamburger topper
11. Vibrating vocal effect
12. Earrings or socks, perhaps
14. Art of folding paper
16. "Caribbean Queen" singer Billy
18. "Days of Our Lives," for one
19. Tart flavor
20. Flip-flops or setbacks

DOWN

1. Its license plates say "Famous Potatoes"
2. Steadfast
3. Look-alike, as in 12-Across
5. Goddess of love and beauty
6. White-knuckled
7. "Bury My Heart at Wounded ___"
10. Hunch or sixth sense
12. Like a romantic evening, maybe
13. Make a pitch for a hitch
15. Plus which
17. Comes closer

Answers on page 177.

PS

ACROSS

1. Questionable
5. Fettuccine, e.g.
8. Cake server, to dieters
9. Friend in Spain
10. Many a Hitchcock film
12. Passover "guest"
14. Teahouse hostess
16. Alfresco eatery
19. "Aida" or "Carmen"
20. Common coffee variety
21. Apache abode
22. Rising current of warm air

DOWN

1. Disliked intensely
2. Famous fawn of film
3. Of like mind
4. Brand owned by Pabst
5. Iridescent string
6. Happy-face symbols
7. Bard of ____ (Shakespeare's nickname)
11. America's pastime
13. "Uncle!"
15. Unoccupied
17. It's accepted as true without proof
18. Capricorn's animal

Answers on page 177.

IN A RUSH

ACROSS

1. Jealous to the max
8. "There ___ to be a law!"
9. Small suitcases
10. University of Wyoming city
11. Grand-scale stories
12. "Voila!"
13. The ego and id are part of it
16. A companion of Porthos
18. Reykjavik's country
20. "I'd rather not discuss it"
21. Chubby Checker's dance
22. Church, mosque or temple

DOWN

1. Halloween spook
2. "Prepare to fence!"
3. "Hurry!"
4. Visible
5. Every which way
6. American of Japanese heritage
7. "Got it"
12. Modeling clay for moppets
14. Telethon's beneficiary
15. So done with
17. Like most people in India
19. Prevent or discourage

Answers on page 178.

DESTINATIONS

ACROSS

1. Bigfoot's other name
6. Thor, Zeus or Athena
8. Dazed and confused
9. Rose stem sticker
10. Bar or oasis
12. Corkscrew pasta
14. Large bird of the Andes
16. Destination not yet determined
19. Fountain in "Three Coins in the Fountain"
20. Army subdivision
21. Like Willie Winkie
22. Downbeat sort

DOWN

1. Like some sale merchandise
2. Tuned to, as a dial
3. Game
4. Wyoming peaks
5. "Rebecca," for one
6. Searched for, in a way
7. Copenhagen native
11. Royal daughter
13. Acrobat's bar
15. Southwest Indian home
17. Clint Eastwood sidekick, in two movies
18. Flight attendant, briefly

Answers on page 178.

CAMPAIGNS AND COMPETITIONS

ACROSS

1. Harasses a comic
5. Nice view
8. Hula-skirt material
9. Cook up
10. Much campaign rhetoric
11. Offshoot
12. Sikh headdress
15. Ties up
18. Cheat on
19. Jaguars and Cougars
20. Hilltop
21. Geometry proposition

DOWN

1. World Court city, with "The"
2. Bell ringer
3. Go broke in Vegas
4. Safe from harm
5. Rattler or cobra
6. Brogans and pumps
7. Craftsman
11. Doubting sort
13. Police journal
14. Ultimatum, for example
16. Skip town to wed
17. ____ salts (bath additive)

Answers on page 178.

PEOPLE AND PLACES

ACROSS

7. "Deadwood" territory
8. Banded marbles
9. "'Twas on the ___ of Capri…"
10. Lab sample for testing
11. "Peekaboo" follower
13. Innocents
15. Tub passenger of rhyme
17. Trumpets and tubas
20. Idaho nickname
21. " Not to mention…"
23. Act the rat
24. Alarms

DOWN

1. Bases, in baseball slang
2. Candy heart line
3. Grandfather, in "Peter and the Wolf"
4. Polished, as a car
5. Boat harbor
6. Look like
12. Key used between words
14. "Green Eggs and Ham" author
16. Bogus
18. Beetle in Egyptian carvings
19. "10,000 ___" (Minnesota license plate slogan)
22. Acorn, essentially

Answers on page 178.

MAPS AND LOCATIONS

ACROSS

1. Their suits come with briefs
4. Amethyst or turquoise
7. "___ obliged!"
8. Rival of Lincoln
9. Baghdad native
11. T ___ tango
13. Google, say
14. Morning mugful
17. Chore list header
19. Absorber of UV rays
22. Take out of commission
23. It's not pretty
24. Blog comments
25. On paper

DOWN

1. Highway posting
2. Kansas's largest city
3. Radio crackling
4. "The Shawshank Redemption" setting
5. "The Island of Doctor Moreau" writer
6. Hunter's need
10. Brow shape
12. Bull's-eye, for Target
13. Web surfer's guide
15. Semi's load
16. Like a jack-o'-lantern
18. Egypt leads the world in their production
20. Check for fit
21. Ancient Egyptians revered it

Answers on page 179.

SAYINGS AND STORIES

ACROSS

1. Twist out of shape
4. Cries like a baby
7. Pass through a crisis safely
8. Like an insufficient account
10. Deny
11. Dinged, as a car
15. Old "March of Time" presentations
16. Sentiment on a sampler
17. Coarse metal files
18. "Huh?"

DOWN

1. Fell
2. Mother Goose offerings
3. Impatience indicator
4. Kodiak or grizzly
5. Milne character who lives inside a tree
6. Abraham's wife, in the Bible
9. Result of an exam
12. Final course, often
13. Candy and such
14. Dislike and then some

Answers on page 179.

BITS AND PIECES

ACROSS

1. Run playfully
5. Entrance into society
8. Clothing fiber at a crime scene, e.g.
9. Soup server's need
10. Fidgety
11. Movie
16. Absorption process
18. Fur tycoon John Jacob
20. Quick as a wink
21. Gather bit by bit, as information
22. Floral wreath

DOWN

1. Avoid a trial, in a way
2. Blue ribbon or gold star
3. It may be under wraps
4. Bridge
5. Guys, slangily
6. Mexican outlaw
7. Giggle sound
12. More than big
13. Walk drunkenly
14. Programmer's job
15. Boxed up
17. Archfiend
19. Oklahoma's "Golden Hurricane"

Answers on page 179.

MOUTH NOISE

ACROSS

1. Jabbers
8. Fish lacking pelvic fins
9. Bikini half
10. Does as one's told
11. Frankness
13. Coffeehouse orders
14. Repeated song part
17. Gentle wind
20. Bullring, for example
21. Part of a circle
22. Aswan or Hoover
23. Hits up for money

DOWN

1. Not at all rigid
2. Reptilian fashion accessory
3. Heavenly
4. Subtle shade
5. Faint, as through ecstasy
6. "Think!"
7. Accessory for Miss Universe
12. 1980s arcade game spinoff
15. Japanese grill
16. Gay Nineties, e.g.
18. Precise
19. Celestial strings

Answers on page 179.

MOVEMENT

ACROSS

1. Woman's sleeveless undergarment
5. "Green ____ and Ham"
8. Jazz standard about an aquatic rodent on a stroll?
9. "60 Minutes" network
10. Unequaled
12. Punch or Judy
14. Wine judge, e.g.
16. Renowned exile
17. "Help wanted" letters
19. Zero in on essentials
20. Diamond corner
21. Makes furious

DOWN

1. Stand-up guy?
2. Buttes' cousins
3. Tanzanian wildlife refuge
4. Long list
6. Pajama party, often
7. Pittsburgh footballer
11. Himalayan hazard
12. Foot-powered taxi
13. Core-strengthening exercises
15. American patriot Hale
17. Swedish autos no longer made
18. Tarot card readers, e.g.

69

Answers on page 180.

WATCH AND PLAY

ACROSS

1. Large trash receptacle
4. Canoe or ferry
8. Cancel
9. Dodge, as a question
10. "Frankenstein" or "Godzilla"
14. Act like a pack rat
15. Inflatable kiddie party rental
18. Love a lot
19. Hannibal's pursuer
20. "Bye," to a Brit
21. Dugong relatives

DOWN

1. "Superman" publisher
2. Cantaloupe or honeydew
3. Cheated
5. Trying to lose
6. High-schooler, usually
7. Comic who plays a supporting role
11. Fully prepared
12. "Emma" updated in a 1995 film
13. Ranger's station
6. "Survivor" group
17. Worm or minnow, perhaps

Answers on page 180.

FOOD AND PHRASES

ACROSS

1. Roll-call discovery
5. Billy-goat feature
7. The Titanic, e.g.
8. Sweetly charming
9. One who keeps dropping things
10. Book copier of yore
12. German leader of yore
15. Carrot sticks, e.g.
18. Very learned
19. Greek sandwiches
20. Salad days
21. Trees, hills, etc.

DOWN

1. Improv line
2. Capitol figure
3. Bungee jumper's requirement
4. Certain former spouse
5. Sudden windfall
6. Part of a bedroom set
10. Wizard's magic
11. Bad spot on a record
13. Blow the budget
14. Classroom break
16. Aquarium nuisance
17. "Cold ____ Tree," Olive Burns novel

Answers on page 180.

FUN PHRASES

ACROSS

1. Fries or coleslaw, typically
8. "Amen, brother!"
9. Classic German camera
10. Squelches early
12. "Nothing runs like a ____" (ad slogan)
14. Company dishes
16. Sealed shut
19. Bavarian souvenir
20. ____ dinner (it's supplied by guests)
21. Nicholson's breakout movie

DOWN

1. Moonlight melody
2. Find, as artifacts
3. Long-shot possibility
4. Give to a fund
5. Carnival thriller
6. Reaction producers
7. "Moby Dick" whaler
11. Knockout punch
13. Plain to see
15. Argentine plains
17. Type of song or trip
18. Aruba or Jamaica

Answers on page 180.

MANY M'S

ACROSS

1. Tasty tidbits
4. Foreboding sign
8. Tom Wolfe's "___ of the Vanities"
9. Backyard barbecue spot
11. Where Glacier National Park is
12. Innocent error
14. Rush-hour woe
16. Censor's sound
18. Frying pan
19. Doc's prescriptions
20. Daniel Boone's state

DOWN

1. Evaporate
2. Weak or uncertain
3. WWII codebreaker
5. Orange-flavored toast spread
6. Tell the story
7. "Charlotte's Web" girl
10. American Theatre Wing prize
12. It flies off store shelves
13. Dramatic side story
15. Carp or flounder
17. Annoying, like a gnat

Answers on page 181.

FOOD AND SYMBOLS

ACROSS

1. "Open sesame!" speaker
5. Avian abodes
8. Extreme greed
9. Sneaky pitch
10. Easily-blamed alter ego
12. Cookie favorite
14. Castle in the air, e.g.
17. 14 pounds, to a Brit
18. Many June babies
19. Items on a "honey-do" list
20. As a large group

DOWN

1. Mexican cliff-diving mecca
2. They're baked in Boise
3. Japanese cartoon art form
4. Bird on a dollar bill
5. Casual Friday rarity
6. Fastest routes (on flat surfaces)
7. Coaster on snow
11. Shimmer iridescently
13. Yesterday's buzz, today
15. 1983 Michael Keaton role-reversal comedy
16. Alternative to "ahem"

Answers on page 181.

PHRASES TO KNOW

ACROSS

1. Apple or cherry place
5. "Playbill" listings
8. Far off
9. Politician's persona
10. Familiar with
12. "I couldn't ____!"
14. Square-dance violin
16. Muscle cramp
19. Hi and bye on Lanai
20. Carry out, as a task
21. Endures
22. Convent group

DOWN

1. "____ People,"
    1980 Oscar winner
2. Is priced at
3. Having a decision to
    make
4. Carbon 14 job
5. Law-enforcement
    officers
6. Like italics
7. Bird feeder tidbit
11. Court officials
13. Groups of fish
15. Some bling
17. "(Get Your Kicks on)
    ____ 66"
18. Cinderella's dance

Answers on page 181.

PASSING THE TIME

ACROSS

1. Horse barns
5. A+ or B-, e.g.
7. Sign of embarrassment
8. Catch forty winks
9. Do this and that
11. Tweak
12. Canal zone
15. Miss America venue, once
19. Hide answers on your hand, say
20. Flagstaff's state
21. Curtains, rugs, etc.
22. Got ready to go out

DOWN

1. Quilter's catchall
2. Dreaded IRS procedure
3. Penny-holding shoes
4. Board with a couple of seats
5. Relish
6. Baseball fan's channel
10. Baltimore's state
13. Records repository
14. Leave isolated
16. Person making a scene?
17. Larger-than-life figures
18. Caustic compound

Answers on page 181.

MANY S'S

ACROSS

1. Invitation to osculation
6. Almost on "E"
8. Clock buzzer
9. Do surgery (on)
10. Be undecided
11. Breaks a road limit
12. Gladiator's protection
15. Uproarious
18. Valuable green stone
19. Folklore dwarf
20. 6-pointers, briefly
21. Has no confidence in

DOWN

1. Butcher's stock
2. City on Puget Sound
3. Kid's sidewalk business
4. Prize on the mantel
5. "Rocky III" theme song
6. Memorize, as lines
7. Time off, for many
11. Whodunit character
13. People people?
14. Windshield wipers
16. Add oil to, maybe
17. Techie sorts

Answers on page 182.

IDENTICAL CHANCES

ACROSS

1. Woman with an inheritance
5. Abacus counters
8. Chancy undertaking
9. Welsh breed
10. Robotic floor vacuum
12. Not crowded
14. "Catch-22" author Heller
17. Panda food
18. Elephant's ivory
21. Identical
22. Abandon, as a project
23. Nags

DOWN

1. Actual money
2. Couch potato, e.g.
3. Rare birds or plants
4. Planet with 62 confirmed moons
6. Nice and friendly
7. Go in search of
11. Chin decor
13. Like a Golden Gloves boxer
15. Wall sockets
16. Beatle-like hairstyle
19. "The final frontier," in "Star Trek"
20. Heifers

Answers on page 182.

TREES AND SLUGS

ACROSS

1. Clam's cousin
4. Hit hard
9. Like the minuet
10. "If the shoe fits, wear it," e.g.
11. "The Simpsons" creator
13. Sandbox scooper
15. Fire-starting stuff
17. Cause of many a blackout
20. Any king
21. Trying to lose
22. Like a $3 bill
23. Handed-down tale

DOWN

1. Hodgepodge
2. Elevator passage
3. Hemlock or spruce
5. Rather sluggish
6. Judge ____ Hand
7. Baby chick's sound
8. Newbies, so to speak
12. Publicized
14. "The Moor of Venice"
16. Evil spirit
18. Martini extra
19. Corn or wheat, collectively

Answers on page 182.

TOYS AND GAMES

ACROSS

1. Musical sound in an aviary
5. "All gone!" sound
8. Kids' game played in a circle
9. Child-lifter's cry?
11. Constitution's Bill of ____
12. Scared
14 Campbell rival
16. Lucky lotto participant
17. Cushy comfort
18. Comes to grips with

DOWN

1. Deputy's shield
2. Some carved Victorian toys
3. Farmer who works the soil, slangily
4. Most pleasant
6. Juice source
7. Like some hippie T-shirts
10. Yellow flowers
11. Lizard or alligator
13. African flying menace
15. Busy month at the IRS

Answers on page 182.

RISKY THINKING

ACROSS

1. Spud from Idaho
4. Outstanding
8. Church high point
9. Broadway legend Merman
10. Take unnecessary risks
11. Plot
16. How innovators need to think
18. Bolt to get hitched
19. Insect with a taste for wood
20. Snickers or Baby Ruth, e.g.
21. Back in the Navy?

DOWN

1. Mathematician Blaise
2. Adjust slightly
3. Peak physical condition
5. Thing on display
6. "Swan Lake", e.g.
7. Luxury option in some cars
12. Squeals on
13. Hard Rock Cafe souvenirs
14. Seriously serious
15. Nonresident doctor
17. Color close to khaki

Answers on page 183.

THE HIGH LIFE

ACROSS

1. Fish of the zodiac
5. Knock down pins in an alley
9. Really resentful
10. Archaeological project
11. Meddle (with)
13. Semifluid, like honey
14. Banded marbles
16. Fahrenheit or Faraday
17. Draw away from shore
19. Words from one on Easy Street, perhaps
20. "Off the Court" author Arthur
21. Kabob stick

DOWN

2. On cloud nine
3. Knowledge
4. Calm and dignified
6. "What's the big rush?"
7. Predicament
8. Halo wearers
12. Very close by
13. Pays a social call
15. Temporary gap
18. Backing-up sound

Answers on page 183.

A GLOBE-SPANNING CAREER

ACROSS

7. Dracula and Basie
8. Fashion designer Laura
9. "10 Things I ___ About You"
10. Nameless
11. Livingstone's discoverer
13. "Encore," literally
15. Vacant
16. For the reason that
18. Maker of the first car radio
19. Mall map word
21. African expedition
22. Jerusalem's land

DOWN

1. "Bridges of Madison County" state
2. Global
3. Made certain
4. Christmas visitor
5. Ones who get the picture
6. Fund-raising events
12. ___ lobe (part of the brain)
14. Terra cotta, for example
17. Get online via password
20. Bassoon or clarinet, e.g.

Answers on page 183.

MISCELLANEOUS

ACROSS

1. Star, on a keyboard
5. Bounders
9. One-year record
10. Nocturnal noisemaker
11. Went separate ways
12. Not more than
13. Word of warning
16. Epithet for Superman
19. Grade, as papers
20. Nez Perce National Forest state
21. Recipe smidgen
22. Suffers in August, perhaps

DOWN

1. A sharp breath
2. Hissy fit
3. Rink rentals
4. Razor inventor Jacob
6. Ancient bazaar
7. "What was I thinking?"
8. Start of a traditional love story
12. Stomach settler
14. Just fair
15. Show deference
17. Brings in, as a salary
18. Birds on Canadian dollars

Answers on page 183.

PATHS AND PERFECTION

ACROSS

1. On the way
8. Early toolmaking period
9. Goof
10. Interstate divider
11. Money and property, e.g.
12. Proposals to buy
15. Bit of hopscotch equipment
18. "Li'l" Dogpatch resident
19. Prom-dress material
20. Stevia's quality

DOWN

1. "Would that it were so!"
2. Farm feeders
3. What a smooth talker has
4. "Soak Up the Sun" singer Crow
5. An ideal match
6. French thanks
7. Gofer's jobs
11. Choose not to vote
13. Display cabinet
14. Like Shelley's skylark
16. Foppish dresser
17. "Grecian Urn" poet

Answers on page 184.

STORIES AND CHARACTERS

ACROSS

1. Ticket given to a bus rider
5. Radiant look
7. Familiar story opener
10. Slope slider
11. What squeaky wheels get
12. No longer hampered by
13. Skin-care brand pitched by Jennifer Aniston
15. Boat's right side
16. Mantra syllables
18. Suspect in Clue
19. Diplomat's talent
20. Marx Brothers forte

DOWN

1. Blows one's horn
2. Florida Keys, e.g.
3. Fall guy in films?
4. French anti-ship missile
6. Cabby's question
8. Italian farewell
9. "Beats me"
12. Hard-to-please sort
14. Place for pedicures and massages
17. Big rigs

Answers on page 184.

MISHMASH

ACROSS

1. Sound of audience approval
5. Actors who overdo it
8. Question from a bartender
9. Halt suddenly
11. Bob of reggae
12. Everglades waders
15. Thin pasta
18. Eider-filled quilt
19. Kate, in "Titanic"
20. Geology and chemistry

DOWN

1. Dam on the Nile
2. Large serving dish
3. Town crier's cry
4. "Sophie's Choice" author
6. Crockett's last battle
7. Detectives
10. Ice cream parlor choice
11. Stroll aimlessly
13. Not consistent
14. Airport pavement
16. Stares openly
17. Computer "infection"

Answers on page 184.

PHRASES AND SAYINGS

ACROSS

1. Pippi Longstocking trademark
4. Alexander Graham Bell, by birth
7. Let up
8. Horses and zebras
11. Bottommost point on the globe
12. Pompous types
14. Camel backbreaker
17. Museum scenic display
18. Appliance company in Iowa
19. Camper owner, for short
20. Sacajawea's tribe

DOWN

1. "The Good Earth" novelist Buck
2. Throat-clearing sounds
3. Committed perjury
5. Wide hallway in a building
6. Cornstalk strands
9. Grunted agreement
10. Gettysburg Address opener
12. More financially sound
13. Holiday, in Italy
15. Prepares, as gifts
16. Bored with it all

Answers on page 184.

A SENSE OF PLACE

ACROSS

1. Legendary reptile with toxic breath
5. Pet rocks, hula hoops, etc.
9. Like chewable bears
10. Hamlet's beloved
11. New Hampshire motto
12. Deserving of merit
13. Scenic views
16. Site of Custer's last stand
19. Miffed
20. After-school helper
21. Emulate Beyonce
22. Having no scent

DOWN

1. Donut-shaped roll
2. Russian urn
3. General situation
4. British biscuits
6. Wasn't well
7. Ushers, for example
8. Streaker in the sky
12. Jitters
14. Harness-race horse
15. Died down
17. Choo-choo
18. Courage or gall

Answers on page 185.

BOOKS AND HOBBIES

ACROSS

1. Hong Kong harbor sights
5. Lowly chess pieces
8. Gulliver's creator
9. New Orleans Saints quarterback
11. Hotel supplies
12. "Hiroshima" author John
14. Well-kept, to a sailor
16. Scene of an Agatha Christie tale
18. Desert drifts
19. Elves, pixies and such

DOWN

1. "Wheel of Fortune" host Pat
2. Perfect shape, in a collectibles ad
3. Class leaders, often
4. Fearful
5. N'est-ce ___?
6. Visibly frightened, perhaps
7. In a manner of speaking
10. Sherlock Holmes in his later years
11. Caught, as a calf
13. West Point students
15. Costume-ball coverings
17. Definite denials

Answers on page 185.

SEARCH AND FIND

ACROSS

1. San Diego Chicken, Mr. Met et al.
5. Hornets and yellowjackets
8. Like a toggle switch
9. John Lennon signature song
10. In close pursuit
11. Capital of Spain
12. Owl, at times
15. Finding-things game
18. Jubilance
19. Like argon or helium
20. New Haven Ivy Leaguer
21. Book before Exodus

DOWN

1. Look for a handout
2. Laughed derisively
3. Quarterback's protectors
4. Slender in build
5. Classic pickup line
6. Paris's river
7. Ceremonial staff
11. Whodunit
13. "Rugs"
14. Christmas drink
16. "___ and the Night Visitors" (Menotti opera)
17. Bags at the mall

Answers on page 185.

DO YOU KNOW THE PHRASE?

ACROSS

1. Fine sweater material
5. Casual talk
9. Pays no mind to
10. Bored feeling
11. Bit of a goof
12. Balanced plank
13. Defendants' excuses
16. Credits for currying favor
19. Archaeologist's find
20. Trellis's crisscross pattern
21. Not up yet
22. Extinguish, as a flame

DOWN

1. Casino stack
2. It may brighten your morning
3. Annual NCAA tournament
4. Get going after a break
6. Temporary tattoo ink
7. Back-of-arm muscle
8. Dodges, as an obligation
12. More than half of Russia
14. Frito ____ (old ad symbol)
15. Camelot wizard
17. Antipasto morsel
18. Animal lure

Answers on page 185.

MODERN LIFE

ACROSS

1. Hilfiger or Lauren
5. Matterhorn's chain
9. Incomplete
10. Get ____ (throw out)
11. In no way ambiguous
12. Wendy's or Subway
14. Forgetful at times
17. "____ on My Pillow" (1958 hit)
18. Stand-up routine, usually
19. Bungee jumping need
20. Don't run with them!

DOWN

1. Andersen or Borge
2. Surgeon's stitches
3. Sheen on some prints
4. Uplifting tunes?
6. Hunter's hangout
7. Paella flavoring
8. Birthday-cake prank
12. Wrought-up
13. Way back when
15. Riser + tread = ____
16. Blues legend Redding

Answers on page 186.

GRAB BAG 2

ACROSS

1. Soft polishing cloth
5. In short supply
8. Chrysler Building's style
9. Camel cousin
10. Lonely, forsaken place
12. Music you don't like
14. Sailor's anchor, maybe
16. Pop
19. "Bye-bye, Brigitte!"
20. Climb with difficulty
21. Power jolt
22. Clergyman's stipend

DOWN

1. Judge's rooms
2. Montezuma's tribe
3. "Be right there!"
4. ___ Doo (cartoon canine)
5. Sailors are known for it
6. In opposition to
7. Boat-deck wood
11. Bathroom fixture
13. Diplomatic messenger
15. Zany
17. Aristocratic
18. Backtalk

Answers on page 186.

VINTAGE PHRASES

ACROSS

1. Ancient scroll material
5. Expertise, informally
8. Bracer
9. Slept on a perch
10. "That's life!"
13. Picturesque
14. Tortilla with meat
16. Junior, for example
18. Country without snakes
19. Sports venue
20. Crude cabin
21. "No worries!"

DOWN

1. Slow-cooked "Yankee" entree
2. Early picture-taker
3. Climbing danger
4. Common ankle injury
6. Cruising
7. Bath bubbles
11. The quetzal is its national bird
12. African anteater
15. Pancho Villa was one
17. Slant or prejudice

Answers on page 186.

COMMON EXPRESSIONS

ACROSS

1. Rustic pipe
5. Clear as a bell
8. Sort of
9. Guard at a post
10. Elaborate dinner
12. "Aloha," in Israel
13. "The Foundation Trilogy" author
17. Apt anagram for Bart
19. "Quiet!"
20. Impending danger, proverbially
21. Greet casually
22. Act of sedition

DOWN

1. Auto body
2. Dome-topped building
3. Passageway
4. Self-serve meal
6. Baked-potato garnish
7. Like London fogs
11. So to speak
14. Genghis Khan's followers
15. Ex-soldier
16. Finger-wagging words
17. Cereal holders
18. Calm, as fears

Answers on page 186.

COMMON IDIOMS

ACROSS

1. Like an A in literature?
5. Pretty suspicious
7. Inactive, as a volcano
8. Dressing choice
9. Breakfast that includes ham, onions and peppers
11. Like string bikinis
13. Iran's former name
15. Robert Penn Warren was the first one in the U.S.
17. Canine restraint
18. More than look up to
19. Highly proficient
20. Spielberg's young treasure hunters

DOWN

1. Fries or slaw, e.g.
2. Chef's garment
3. "Enough on this subject"
4. Bugle call
5. Query at a fast-food counter
6. Dojo masters
10. Cornish delicacies
12. Hawaiian farewell song
14. Indy activity
16. Lardner's "___ Ike"

Answers on page 187.

MIXED BAG

ACROSS

1. Feel-good campfire song
5. Intoxicating, as perfume
7. Luthor, to Superman
8. "Bye, hombre"
9. Rock used for hammering, e.g.
11. Mark of prestige
13. Chiquita of old commercials
15. Idyllic vacation spot
17. "On easy street," e.g.
18. Crunchy salad morsel
19. Ball of yarn or flock of geese in flight
20. Chew the scenery

DOWN

1. Backpack relative
2. Chinese gambling mecca
3. Ubiquitous Mad Magazine guy
4. Get payback for
5. Family circle
6. Tombstone locale
10. Dry red wine
12. Loose-fitting undergarment
14. Exterior masonry finish
16. Early capital of Alaska

Answers on page 187.

FOOD AND MUSIC

ACROSS

1. Intolerant Seuss creature
5. "Taras Bulba" author Nikolai
8. Follower
9. "Carmen" or "Rigoletto"
10. Milky Way, for one
12. Artist known for spatial illusions
14. Carson City is its capital
15. Outdoor eatery
19. Bit of improvisation
20. Boardwalk locale
21. Aid in finding sunken ships
22. Fast train

DOWN

1. Decorator's samples
2. ___ Lodge (motel chain)
3. "The Fantasticks" classic
4. "Laughing" scavenger
5. Adjustable desktop light
6. 1983 U.S. invasion site
7. Alchemist's raw material
11. Like a wallflower
13. Relaxin', slangily
16. Airline seat choice
17. Close to identical
18. "Memory" musical

Answers on page 187.

POTPOURRI

ACROSS

1. Era that began with Sputnik
5. Crosswalk, on signs
8. Biblical floating zoo
9. Float in the air
10. Stretch of low-temperature days
14. From dawn to dusk
15. Take to the air
17. Goose-bumps feeling
20. Call from the deck
21. Proceed with gusto
22. Like a runt
23. Knight's weapon

DOWN

1. Measure of passing time
2. Moby Dick's pursuer
3. Place to sit in the den
4. Use a mouthwash
6. Bold challenge
7. "Dude, move on!"
11. Underestimate
12. Final critical moment
13. A very long time
16. Creased hat
18. Drift off
19. "Goldfinger" fort

Answers on page 187.

ASSORTMENT

ACROSS

1. Tub of hydrotherapy
5. Virtual hailing service
8. "When pigs fly!"
9. Coffee or island
11. The dating scene, to some
14. "Holy" Ohio town
15. French city on the Channel
17. Spies may go behind them
20. Former significant others
21. "Not to mention…"
22. Theater offering
23. Inextricably involved

DOWN

1. Move in the breeze
2. Teensy-weensy
3. What a threadbare coat may have seen
4. BLT ingredient
6. Bad omen, to some
7. Driver's license hurdle
10. Event for unloading junk
12. Vatican City basilica
13. A second self
16. Cry uncle
18. Standup bit
19. "Beetle Bailey" vehicle

Answers on page 188.

CROSSWORD COLLECTION

ACROSS

1. Bucket list list
5. Comes to the rescue of
8. "All ___ Eve"
9. Anna Moses' nickname
10. Allegro or andante, e.g.
11. Authorize
12. Authored
14. Didn't just simmer
17. Do an impression of
19. Activates a beeper
21. Changed to fit in
22. In the neighborhood
23. The Riddler, to Batman
24. All shook up

DOWN

1. "Rough" edition
2. Guys who always get black eyes?
3. 3:1, e.g.
4. "Send up a ___, I'll throw you a line" (Billy Joel lyric)
5. 1975 Beatty-Hawn film
6. YouTube upload
7. Agar source
12. Not open to the public
13. "Bingo!"
15. Based on reason
16. "See Spot run" book
18. Handler's concern
19. Cockpit figure
20. "Crazy ___," Ephron book

Answers on page 188.

WHAT DID YOU SAY?

ACROSS

1. Closing number
4. Holiday, in Napoli
8. Decorating theme
9. Knocked to the ground
10. Setting increased standards
11. Sitting Bull's tribe
12. Clan pattern
15. Six Flags or Disneyland
18. Encomium
19. Happy Meals toy, e.g.
20. Bloodhound trail
21. Grade-school outside break

DOWN

1. Longest bone in the body
2. Criticize the small stuff
3. Overtaken and easily surpassed
4. Thoroughly
5. Abort, as a mission
6. Fireplace log holder
7. 18 or 21, usually
11. Makeshift shelters
13. Circus acrobat's swing
14. Army Ranger's topper
16. Become one
17. Sovereigns

Answers on page 188.

MISHMASH 2

ACROSS

1. Minor battle
5. Army food
9. Cattle thief
10. Boot out, as a tenant
11. Pointer (often ignored)
12. Get together
13. Potential wild cards
16. Group behind many a roast
19. "Star Wars" good guys
20. Embarrassment
21. Biting remark
22. They make miniatures

DOWN

1. Flapjack topper
2. Look over carefully
3. Fireman's badge shape
4. Place to pick up a kitten
6. Creole-speaking nation
7. 1985 film set in Amish country
8. World leaders
12. Found work
14. Blow up, as a picture
15. Pampas cowboy
17. Influential tribe member
18. Christmas bonanza

Answers on page 188.

RANDOM KNOWLEDGE

ACROSS

1. Says "My bad!"
5. Contragate bits
9. Polar cover
10. Disney's Montana
11. Nightclub employees
12. Classic Harlem theater
15. Overused routine
20. Ceramics artisan
21. Global conflict
22. Have the desired result
23. Cut to fit
24. Recruit deceptively
25. Graf once of tennis

DOWN

2. Home of the slender-waisted
3. Broadway opening
4. Chemical used in soap
5. "Uh" sounds
6. Chosen by chance
7. Devil, in Durango
8. Students' publication
13. What every worker wants
14. Goes first
16. Treasure city, with "El"
17. Good-for-nothing
18. Potatoes au ____
19. Lawn mower paths

Answers on page 189.

ARBITRARILY

ACROSS

1. Willed property
4. What former foes make
9. Like most new drivers
10. Tot's three-wheeler
11. 1960 Rat Pack comedy
13. Procrastinator's reply
15. Plot
17. Lacking moral principles
20. Garlicky mayo
21. New England football pro
22. Brief race
23. Side roads

DOWN

1. Disappointments
2. V formation members
3. Falling-domino effect
5. Homeland
6. Innocent nature
7. Champagne flute part
8. Floppy topper
12. Internet locations
14. "Roger"
16. Aquarium staple
18. Board for a seance
19. Preserves, as food

Answers on page 189.

MUSIC AND FOOD

ACROSS

1. Erases
5. African antelope
9. Apache leader
10. Dramatist O'Neill
11. Inactivity
12. Connecting strips
15. Dessert topping
20. Drop by
21. Showing off
22. Chess ploy
23. Edible parts of pecans
24. Fancy serving tray
25. Fab Four manager Brian

DOWN

1. Like a rascal
2. Pear variety
3. Coming clean
4. Meter indicator, in music
6. Chilled dessert
7. Motown's Franklin
8. Kind of acid in vinegar
13. Destructive waves
14. Sticky stuff on stamps
16. Bitter oranges
17. Dress-up affair
18. Like intervention from above
19. Enters carefully

Answers on page 189.

JOHN GOTTI

ACROSS

1. Airport boarding area
5. One of Gotti's nicknames was "____ Don"
11. Difficult skating jump
12. Court crier's words
13. Get a new loan, slangily
14. Had a debate
15. Big initials in fashion
16. Annual stage award since 1956
17. "Good Vibrations" or "Surfin' Safari"
19. C.S.A. soldier
22. Assembly of church officials
24. Far from fresh
26. Final musical passage
27. As high as you can get
28. Tag ____ with (accompany)
30. Big name in cameras
31. Day of many a Fed. holiday
32. Familiar fruit logo
34. Aspersion
35. Golf peg

38. Obi Wan, to Luke
41. Breakfast or lunch
42. Nicholson's threesome
43. It's more, in a saying
44. Baby's knitwear
45. La ____ Tar Pits

DOWN

1. Cooper of "High Noon"
2. Cabin builders' need
3. After three acquittals, Gotti came to be known as the ____
4. Yale grad
5. Oil emirate Abu ____
6. Eagles' nests
7. Book leaf
8. Boston skyscraper, informally, with "the"
9. Daisy center
10. Crimson or scarlet
16. Curious
18. Advance from a shark
19. Capone, e.g., or Gotti
20. "Sesame Street" ticklee
21. Existed
22. A Ponzi scheme is one
23. Texter's "carpe diem"

25. Suspect's shadow
29. Aplenty
30. "All Things Considered" carrier
33. Change holder
34. Now, in the ICU
36. Comfortable situation
37. "Frozen" belle

38. Capo's crowd
39. "___ Beso" ("That Kiss," Anka hit)
40. Drill sgt. e.g.
41. Org. for the Boys of Summer

Answers on page 189.

THE UNABOMBER

ACROSS
1. Drink often served with sushi
5. Like most streets
11. Mongolia's ___ Bator
12. Balzac's first name
13. Four-sided fig.
14. Safer time to eat oysters, supposedly
15. Moroccan headwear
16. Shirts with pictures on them
17. Arab Spring country
19. Benchmark: Abbr.
22. Mount that Moses climbed
24. Kipling tiger ___ Khan
26. Bonnie belle
27. Egg-shaped
28. Good way to sing
30. Deplane dramatically
31. It comes between chi and omega
32. It merged with Mobil in 1999
34. Float gently in the air
35. Brief "despite"
38. Olympic skater Ito
41. Doc's prescriptions
42. Dead Sea artifact
43. It means "beyond"
44. Hippie-style pattern
45. "Green-eyed monster"

DOWN
1. Catch a wave
2. Out of the wind, at sea
3. The Unabomber was revealed to be former math teacher Ted ___
4. "The Lord of the Rings" tree creature
5. Babe Ruth's number
6. French's "The ___ Room"
7. Sean and Yoko
8. Came in first place
9. Getty Museum pieces
10. Casual "Sure"
16. "Didn't need to hear that!"
18. Move without effort
19. Number of years the Unabomber eluded authorities
20. Gillette ___ II razor

21. Bench press muscle, slangily
22. Chow for a sow
23. Authors Fleming and McEwan
25. Orange-roofed chain, familiarly
29. Like some checkups
30. Abbr. after a telephone no.
33. Case for Mulder and Scully
34. Authorities said Kaczynski's use of ___ seemed to be an obsession
36. Modern viewing option, for short
37. Anthem opener
38. Ariz. setting all year round
39. French for "here"
40. Beats By Dr. ___
41. Bovary's brief title

Answers on page 190.

WATERGATE

ACROSS
1. Breakfast drink
6. Building girder
11. Fur trader John Jacob
12. Beef casing
13. The threat of impeachment led to Nixon's ___
15. "One more thing"
16. Are, in the past
17. Physiques, informally
19. Society-column word
21. Charlottesville campus, for short
22. Nixon took steps to ___ the Watergate scandal
26. Release one's grip
28. Kin on mother's side
29. Five "burglars" were involved in the Watergate ___
31. The "p" of mph
32. "Read Across America" grp.
33. Cousin of "ahem"
34. Soothing lotion
37. Capricorn's animal
39. Washington Post reporters ___ and Carl Bernstein uncovered Watergate details
43. To the back
44. How losses are often shown
45. Emerald's mineral
46. Hairpin curves

DOWN
1. Bottle for pickles
2. Exhaust, with "up"
3. "See you then!"
4. Mattress springs
5. Energy units
6. Ore-___ Tater Tots
7. Betwixt and ___
8. Lake that sounds spooky
9. Bow-wielding deity
10. Hair on a lion's neck
14. Taboo to a toddler
17. Tulip-to-be
18. Eggs ___ easy
20. Tied, as a score
22. Popular pop
23. Jay-Z, LL Cool J and others

24. All-purpose trucks, informally
25. Chipper and frisky
27. Vessel's temporary bridge
30. "Aladdin" parrot
33. Chessboard sixteen
34. Common rhyme scheme

35. Body of tradition
36. Above, in Germany
38. "Garfield" beagle
40. The NBA's Magic on scoreboards
41. Mr. ___ (old detective game)
42. Dentist's deg.

Answers on page 190.

MARTIN SCORSESE MOVIES

ACROSS

1. Big bashes
6. CEO degrees
10. Woolly animal at a petting zoo
11. A psychic may see one
12. What the Sup. Court interprets
13. Eye part that contains color
14. 1990 De Niro gangster film directed by Martin Scorsese
16. Museum paintings
17. Filming location
20. Soap opera hunk, say
24. "How are you?" reply
26. Troop's camping place
27. 1975 De Niro film directed by Martin Scorsese
29. "To ___ own self be true": Shak.
30. Crime-solving Wolfe
31. Highwayman
33. Put in words
34. Buccaneer's bounty
36. 1980 De Niro film about a boxer, directed by Martin Scorsese
42. Plate with five sides
43. Carrie in "Carrie"
44. Manages, with "out"
45. Forearm bones
46. Isn't wrong?
47. Municipal maps

DOWN

1. Water cooler sound
2. "And another thing…"
3. Schifrin who wrote the "Mission: Impossible" theme
4. Brazilian novelist Jorge
5. Deemed appropriate
6. Performs halfheartedly, slangily
7. Balladeer Ives
8. "Elsa's Dream" is one
9. Backtalk
15. Young eel
17. Degree in letters
18. Beach at Normandy
19. Natural poison
21. Barry and Brubeck

22. "Aida" or "Tosca"
23. "Bad, Bad" Brown of song
25. Most considerate
28. NFL Hall of Famer Sanders
32. Gets dressed
35. Govt. note
36. Ostrich-like bird
37. Golf Hall of Famer Isao
38. Feds
39. Annapolis campus: Abbr.
40. Aspiring D.A.'s exam
41. Caustic soaps

Answers on page 190.

MAKING A MURDERER

ACROSS

1. Supporting timber
6. Brew in a teapot
11. Happen
12. Buzzy abodes
13. Subject of Netflix true crime series
15. Bladed pole
16. Aviation: prefix
17. Narrow winning margin
18. Blasting inits.
21. Dances like Cinderella's
24. Bad place for a roller skate
26. Lincoln and Vigoda
27. "Grand Theft ___" (video game)
28. Continue, as a subscription
30. Surprise win
31. Little green men, for short
32. Sooners' st.
34. Halloween shouts
35. Dish from taro root
38. Forensic evidence found in a car
42. Phobias
43. Give the boot
44. Like an area filled with fronds
45. Witherspoon of "Legally Blonde"

DOWN

1. "Believe" singer Groban
2. Prefix for eight
3. Big name in slushes
4. Soccer mom's vehicle
5. Radial patterns
6. Stock-market units
7. Record for later, in a way
8. First lady
9. Bard's "ever"
10. "Gangnam Style" performer
14. Photo orig.
17. Otherwise
18. Cross-shaped letters
19. Dark time, in ads
20. Bouncy pace
21. Like a fairy-tale cupboard
22. Act as lookout, say
23. Eyeglass part

25. Barcelona bar bite
29. Like pine scent, perhaps
30. Long, heavy overcoat
33. Bout stoppers, briefly
34. "____ in the U.S.A." (Springsteen hit)
35. King Cole's request

36. Wallet bills
37. Gilligan's spot
38. Closest pal, in text
39. "Life of Pi" director Ang
40. Kayaker's need
41. Bunyan's tool

Answers on page 190.

FBI MOST WANTED

ACROSS

1. Journalists, collectively
6. Place to dissect frogs
12. "Guitar Town" guitarist Steve
13. Baseball official
14. Easy as can be
15. Comics jungle queen
16. First person on the Most Wanted list (1950); shot to death his wife and her two brothers in 1949.
18. Group of very minor celebs
19. Belle's boyfriend
22. Rule of conduct
27. NBA and PGA, for two
29. Drop by on a whim
30. 1964 movie about a heist in an Istanbul museum
33. "Cool," to Ice-T
34. Allow to pass
36. The famed bank robber was #11 on the list (1950).
43. Handed out, as a citation
44. Big horned beast, briefly
45. California senator Feinstein
46. French film director Louis
47. Fancy house and grounds
48. Lawyers: Abbr.

DOWN

1. Bog moss
2. Aloe vera target
3. Cube creator Rubik
4. Dramatic basket
5. Flower part
6. Pres. before Clinton
7. Mummy in "The Mummy"
8. Audi rival
9. Perjured oneself
10. "Rule Britannia" composer
11. "String" veggie
17. Drink like a lady
19. Belfry resident
20. "___ Beso" ("That Kiss," Anka hit)

21. Cleo's cobra
23. "I understand" in radio lingo
24. N.T. book written by Paul
25. "Hairspray" actress Zadora
26. "Rizzoli & Isles" channel
28. Prominent, as a feature
31. Carolinas river
32. The "I" in TGIF

35. Myanmar's old name
36. Like a mason jar's mouth
37. Egyptian nature goddess
38. Atty.-to-be's exam
39. Beautiful moth
40. Pinball aborter
41. "We've ___ Just Begun" (1970 Carpenters song)
42. Con votes

Answers on page 191.

FAMOUS UNSOLVED CRIMES

ACROSS

1. Wrist-related
7. Not as much
11. Vehicle pulled by yoked animals
12. Formally relinquish
13. Authorities have never solved the grisly murder of 22-year-old Elizabeth Short, dubbed the ___
15. Baryshnikov nickname
16. Companion of Kukla and Ollie
18. Mozart's "___ Kleine Nachtmusik"
21. Caramel-glazed custard
22. The death of 6-year-old beauty queen JonBenet ___ still baffles police
24. A billion years, in geology
25. Crosswalk user, briefly
26. First word of "Scarborough Fair"
27. The ___ Killer murdered five people, taunted cops with cryptic clues, but was never caught

29. Jacob who wrote "How the Other Half Lives"
30. "Falling Into You" singer Celine
31. Iranian forebear
32. Enlarge, as a road
34. The 1996-97 deaths of rapper ___ and his rival Biggie Smalls remain unsolved
40. It may be a bad sign
41. Ineffective
42. Breaks in continuity
43. Sickly, as a complexion

DOWN

1. Corn eater's discard
2. Guns N' Roses singer Rose
3. Co. that formed NBC
4. Binky and Pinky's game
5. "Argo" actor Alan
6. Fords often used as cop cars
7. "Fiddler on the Roof"toast
8. Unagi, in a sushi bar

9. Reagan pet project: Abbr.
10. Swell place?
14. Good way to plan
16. Monsoon result, often
17. "Amazing" illusionist
19. Ibuprofen, e.g.
20. Like theremin noises, usually
21. Casablanca cap
22. "Parks and ___" (NBC series)
23. Last word of "Ulysses"
25. Stampede cause
28. Hawkeye State residents
29. Fix, as a loose board
31. Conductor Zubin
33. Brit. military awards
34. Dress fancily, with "out"
35. "Kill Bill" actress Thurman
36. High energy
37. ___ Nidre, Hebrew prayer
38. Bob Hope tour grp.
39. VCR back-up button

1	2	3	4	5	6	■	7	8	9	10
11						■	12			
13						14				
■	■		15					■	■	■
■	16	17			■	18		19	20	■
21				■	22				23	
24			■	25			■	26		
27			28			■	29			
■	30				■	31			■	■
■			32		33				■	■
34	35	36					■	37	38	39
40				■	41					
42				■	43					

Answers on page 191.

CHICAGO P.D.

ACROSS

1. Police Det. Jay Halstead is played by ____ Lee Soffer
6. NASA's domain
11. Maker of electric brushes
12. "The Planets" composer Gustav
13. Some old iPods
14. Hip-related
15. Word in a kid's counting rhyme
17. He's Det. Sgt. Hank Voigt on "Chicago P.D."
22. Austrian peak
23. Ladies, in old gangster films
25. J. ____ Band
28. Like a catty remark
29. Predicament
31. Kit ____ (Hershey brand)
32. She's Police Det. Erin Lindsay on "Chicago P.D."
35. Bandleader Goodman
36. Irate feeling
39. More than eccentric
43. Canada's national tree
44. Muslim moguls
45. "Sailing to Byzantium" poet
46. Cars the bank takes back

DOWN

1. Senior Police Det. Antonio Dawson is played by ____ Seda
2. Newsworthy time
3. Japanese name suffix
4. Certain replay
5. "Barnaby Jones" actor Buddy
6. Fistfight souvenirs
7. Many-sided figure
8. "Aladdin" hero
9. Gp. whose military wore gray
10. List ender, for short
16. Flow back, as a tide
17. Sporty English autos
18. Guinness and Baldwin
19. Agnew who resigned
20. Japanese terse verse
21. Icelandic sagas

24. Meyers of late-night
26. Plane seat restraint
27. Areas of influence
30. German's one
33. Actress Gabrielle ____
34. How toys may be rated

36. Sgt. Trudy Platt is played by ____ Morton
37. Highlands negative
38. 4.0 is a good one
40. West Coast hwy. cop
41. Police Det. Sheldon Jin is played by Archie ____
42. 1940s spy grp.

1	2	3	4	5		6	7	8	9	10
11						12				
13						14				
			15		16					
17	18	19						20	21	
22					23					24
25			26	27		28				
29					30			31		
	32					33	34			
		35								
36	37	38				39		40	41	42
43						44				
45						46				

Answers on page 191.

CHARLES MANSON

ACROSS

1. Peter Max genre
7. Preparing for combat
13. Irregular in quality
14. Deli patron's request
15. What Manson called his macabre killing plan, borrowing the 1968 Beatles song
17. Length x width, for a rectangle
18. Auto club inits.
19. Inactive: Abbr.
20. '40s Treasury issue
22. Like boring writing
24. "Shoo!"
25. Baby goat sound
26. Faun-like deity
29. Had regrets
33. 1996 Olympic torch lighter
34. Totally control
35. Brass band boomer
36. Manson, a musician, named his 1970 album "Lie: The ____ Cult"
40. 1912 Olympics star Jim
41. Out jogging
42. Gets smart with
43. Transfers a rootbound begonia, say

DOWN

1. "Fiddlesticks!"
2. "Tosca" or "Carmen"
3. Gondola mover
4. "Way to go, guy!"
5. 1 or 66, e.g.
6. Dictatorial ruler
7. "Crazy Love" singer Paul
8. Beluga eggs
9. 2050, in old Rome
10. Physician: Comb. form
11. Moscow negatives
12. Berry of Motown
16. Feeling blue
21. "____ Town": Wilder
22. Good buddy
23. Dilapidated digs
25. Trusted adviser
26. Epsom and the like
27. Island welcome
28. Records for laterviewing, colloquially
29. E-mail directive: Abbr.

30. Grand Canyon pack animal
31. In the area
32. Does some mending
34. Low bills
37. Places to see M.D.'s in a hurry
38. Donkey Kong or King Kong
39. Direction from L.A. to N.Y.

1	2	3	4	5	6		7	8	9	10	11	12
13							14					
15						16						
17					18					19		
20				21				22	23			
			24				25					
26	27	28				29				30	31	32
33					34				35			
36			37	38				39				
40							41					
42							43					

Answers on page 191.

BROOKLYN NINE-NINE

ACROSS

1. With 29-Across, he's Capt. Raymond Holt on "Brooklyn Nine-Nine"
6. 100 clams
11. "The Three Musketeers" author
12. Took a bead on
13. He plays Jake Peralta on "Brooklyn Nine-Nine"
15. Blacken, as a steak
16. Big brother of the SAT
17. Melissa Fumero is ___ Santiago on "Brooklyn Nine-Nine"
20. Opposes
22. Restrained, as a Rottweiler
24. It's just not done
25. Excellent rating
29. See 1-Across
33. Museum display
36. ___ culpa (my bad)
37. Conquistador's gold
38. Emeril Lagasse sounds
40. He's Michael Hitchcock on "Brooklyn Nine-Nine"
45. "Grumpy Old Men" actor Davis
46. Dirty, as a chimney
47. Butler of "Gone With the Wind"
48. How often Santa checks his list

DOWN

1. 1969 Nabokov novel
2. Mother Teresa, notably
3. Dentist's deg.
4. Beta and gamma
5. Dead Sea monastic
6. Some Toyotas
7. Mont Blanc tip
8. Last letter of the Greek alphabet
9. ___ Crews is Sgt. Jeffords on "Brooklyn Nine-Nine"
10. A sphere lacks them
14. Laser pointer battery size
17. ___ Center (Chicago skyscraper)
18. 6 on a cell phone
19. PBS chef Martin

21. Casually catch flies
23. Ear or leaf feature
26. Elec. unit
27. "Born," in some notices
28. Part of an eon
30. Carpentry groove
31. Kazakh sea that's basically a desert now
32. Greatest degree
33. Travel guide publisher
34. Kind of stew or whiskey
35. From Oslo, e.g.
39. Bargelike boat
41. Hobby shop put-together
42. Colorful carp
43. Latin list ender
44. Bread used for a Reuben

Answers on page 192.

BLUE BLOODS

ACROSS

1. A bit damp
6. Hook or Cook: Abbr.
10. Split apart
11. Take on, as employees
12. Movie trailer exhortation
13. "… lovin' the spin ___"
14. He's Police Commissioner Frank Reagan
16. Grinning emoticons
17. Agent Gold of "Entourage"
20. Brand on many an auto racer's jacket
21. Young chaps
23. "Dinner at ___"
27. Danny Reagan's wife who was killed in a helicopter crash
29. Paintball impact sound
30. Lively tune
31. Org. that owns WorldSeries.com
33. "Hollywood Squares" symbols
34. It beats an ace
38. She's feisty Officer "Eddie" Janko, Jamie Reagan's fiancée
42. Jewish calendar's twelfth month
43. Cliched
44. Gold cloth
45. Affix a new price to
46. Arrived feet-first
47. Ape from Borneo, briefly

DOWN

1. "Gorillas in the ___," 1988 film
2. "___'Clock Jump" (Basie theme)
3. Couple in a gossip column
4. "The ___ Family Robinson"
5. Aboriginal emblems
6. Metaphorical prescription for one in a tizzy
7. "A Man and a Woman" actress
8. Big-ticket

9. Distance races
15. About a quarter of a gallon
17. Cry said with a sigh
18. Expressway exit
19. Charming scene
22. Played tag, e.g.
24. E.U. group
25. Pail problem
26. Blows up with| explosives

28. Trip planner's aid
32. Chic eatery
34. Egg outlines
35. Tennis champ Rafael
36. As a friend, in France
37. More desirable to collectors
39. "Lovely ___" (Beatles song)
40. ___ angle (obliquely)
41. B-movie baddie

Answers on page 192.

BERNIE MADOFF

ACROSS

1. Bakery come-on
6. "The ___ Mutiny" (Bogart film)
11. Armstrong of jazz
12. Speed up, in music: Abbr.
13. Madoff's "epic fraud" was a ___
15. Bailout computer key
16. Took a load off
17. Drink, for short
18. "Hollaback Girl" singer Gwen
20. Suffix for Nepal or Siam
21. Dishonest response
22. 2000 Oscar role for Julia
23. '60s TV horse
25. Batting nos.
26. Enjoy the library
27. Hindu title of respect
28. Ballpark figure, briefly
29. Regular haunt
33. Center of a simile
34. Foe of Frazier and Foreman
35. Neighbor of Neb.
36. The loss to many of Madoff's thousands of victims
39. Puts in the letter box
40. "Skyfall" singer
41. "I have left a legacy of ___," Madoff admitted to his victims
42. Not as high

DOWN

1. French peaks, to the French
2. Avian hangout
3. Part of a pound
4. "Les ___" (Broadway musical)
5. "Let me repeat…"
6. Cholla and saguaro
7. "Alas!" in Austria
8. Titanic sinker
9. Moriarty, to Holmes
10. Madoff was convicted of ___ federal felonies
14. All there upstairs
19. Cut and run

22. Federal judge Denny Chin called Madoff's crimes "extraordinarily ___"
23. Handel masterwork
24. Almond liqueur
25. Airport listing
26. Kingly domains
27. Toni Morrison novel
29. Behind the times
30. "You didn't have to tell me"
31. Colonel insignia
32. Al or Bobby of racing
37. Boat-building wood
38. Affirmative at the altar

Answers on page 192.

AMERICAN SERIAL KILLERS

ACROSS

1. Goblet, e.g.
6. Eye rudely
11. Record-company name
12. "No more procrastinating!"
13. Sports venue
14. Fully up-to-date
15. Rodney Alcala was called the "___ ___ Killer" because he appeared on the game show in the midst of his killing spree
17. Playful river critter
18. Early stage of life
21. A bit wet
25. Fan's rebuke
26. Grumpy colleague?
27. Dinghy or canoe
29. "___ Fables"
32. Kind of bird or riser
34. John Norman Collins was known as the "___ ___"
39. Japanese meal in a box
40. Like sheep
41. Beneath, in Berlin
42. Country star Tucker
43. Brick-and-mortar operation
44. "Slammin' Sammy" of golf

DOWN

1. Happy or content
2. "Doctor Zhivago" heroine
3. Act as a lookout, e.g.
4. Graduate-to-be
5. Like italic type
6. Performer's platform
7. In the direction of
8. Eden evacuee
9. Almost never seen
10. Hole in a needle
16. '60s Pontiac muscle car
18. Flow out
19. "Got milk?" comeback, perhaps
20. Anaconda's cousin
22. Fuss and feathers
23. Hard-to-comb hair
24. Many computers
28. Balance unsteadily

29. Floating biblical sanctuary
30. George and T.S.
31. Very wooded
33. Go gaga over
34. It won't buy much

35. Fully aware of
36. Fishing cord
37. "A Day Without Rain" singer
38. Enjoy a magazine
39. Clear tables and such

Answers on page 192.

ANSWERS

Time and Magic (Page 4)

Osteology (Page 8)

Science and Nature (Page 6)

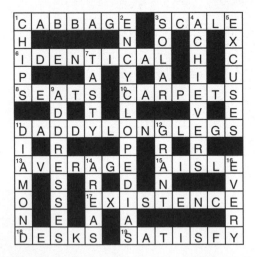

Jobs and Industries (Page 10)

Miscellany (Page 12)

Phrases for a Road Trip (Page 16)

A Glitzy Lifestyle (Page 14)

Stories and Sayings (Page 18)

Grab Bag (Page 20)

Vivid Phrases (Page 24)

Evocative Phrases (Page 22)

Money and Mount Olympus (Page 26)

Oxymorons (Page 28)

Places and Events (Page 32)

Predictions and Forecasts (Page 30)

Common Phrases (Page 34)

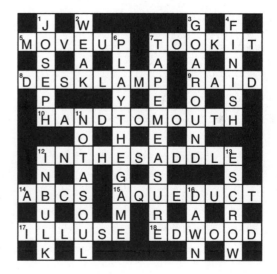

Melange (Page 36)

```
S W I S S G U A R D ■
A V N S I C
L L A M A F I T S I N
E N K L Z C M
S P A C E B A R W A C O
P P G B D B
I D I D I T S A F A R I
T N T W D L
C O A X W H I T E L I E
H W P Y A A H
H A V E O N S A N T O
Y S O T A M
T O E T H E L I N E
```

Characters and Phrases (Page 40)

```
M A A N D P A K E T T L E
A S E P S X
R A T R A C E S H E E P
I R D M L O
A B O D E A C A C I A S
Y N O E
C R A N E S C A C T U S
L G P B
A W E S O M E O P A L S
S S E L N A
S A A B S W A I K I K I
I G E S S L
C O O L O N E S H E E L S
```

Hodgepodge (Page 38)

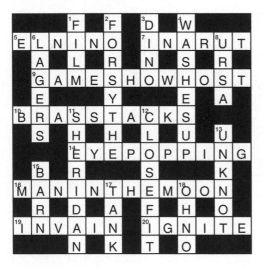

```
F F D W
E L N I N O I N A R U T
A L R N S R
G A M E S H O W H O S T
E Y E A
B R A S S T A C K S
S H H L U U
E Y E P O P P I N G
B R S K
M A N I N T H E M O O N
R D A F H O
I N V A I N I G N I T E
N K T O
```

Competition and Conflict (Page 42)

```
P R O S A I C A I N S
A A L N A
C R I M S O N T I D E F
K C A X E
A C H E S A S S A I L
B S N L B
A U S S I E C A M E T O
G E O O A
B A Z A A R B E A T S
F T D N T
T R O J A N H O R S E
L B T R
A X E E E C L A I R S
```

Avoidance Tactics (Page 44)

Double Vision (Page 48)

Food and Sleep (Page 46)

PS (Page 50)

In a Rush (Page 52)

Campaigns and Competitions (Page 56)

Destinations (Page 54)

People and Places (Page 58)

178

Maps and Locations (Page 60)

Across/Down grid solution:
- LAWYERS · JEWEL
- MUCH · CADILLAC
- IRAQI · ASIN
- SEARCH · COFFEE
- TODO · OZONE
- MOTHBALL · UGLY
- POSTS · WRITTEN

Bits and Pieces (Page 64)

Grid solution:
- SCAMPER · DEBUT
- TRACEEVIDENCE
- LADLE · RESTIVE
- PICTURESHOW
- OSMOSIS · ASTOR
- INNOTHINGFLAT
- GLEAN · GARLAND

Sayings and Stories (Page 62)

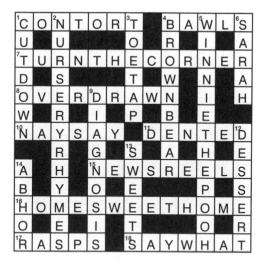

Grid solution:
- CONTORT · BAWLS
- TURNTHECORNER
- OVERDRAWN
- NAYSAY · DENTED
- A · NEWSREELS
- HOMESWEETHOME
- RASPS · SAYWHAT

Mouth Noise (Page 66)

Grid solution:
- FLAPSONESGUMS
- EEL · BRA · OBEYS
- CANDOR
- LATTES · CHORUS
- BREEZE
- ARENA · ARC · DAM
- PUTSTHEBITEON

Movement (Page 68)

Food and Phrases (Page 72)

Watch and Play (Page 70)

Fun Phrases (Page 74)

Many M's (Page 76)

```
D A I N T I E S   O M E N
R     E   N   F A   A   A
Y   B O N F I R E   R   R
U     U   G   R   M   R
P A T I O   M O N T A N A
    O   U   A       L   T
H O N E S T M I S T A K E
O   Y       A   U   D
T R A F F I C   B L E E P
I   W   I   H   P       E
T   A   S K I L L E T   S
E   R   H   N   O       K
M E D S   K E N T U C K Y
```

Phrases to Know (Page 80)

```
O R C H A R D   C A S T S
R O T   A   R   L   E
D I S T A N T   I M A G E
I   T   C   I   M   N   D
N O S T R A N G E R T O
A   O   G   F   E     R
R E S I S T   F I D D L E
Y   C   S   J   G       F
  C H A R L E Y H O R S E
B O   O   W   T   O   R
A L O H A   E X E C U T E
L   L   D   L   R   T   E
L A S T S   S I S T E R S
```

Food and Symbols (Page 78)

```
A L I B A B A   N E S T S
C   D   N   M   E   T   L
A V A R I C E   C U R V E
P   H   M   R   K   A   D
U   O   E V I L T W I N
L   P   C   I   G   O
C H O C O L A T E C H I P
O   T   L   N   T   I   A
  D A Y D R E A M   L   L
P   T   N   A   R   I   E
S T O N E   G E M I N I S
S   E   W   L   O   E   C
T A S K S   E N M A S S E
```

Passing the Time (Page 82)

```
S T A B L E S   G R A D E
C   U   O   E   U       S
R E D F A C E   S L E E P
A   I   F   S   T       N
P U T T E R A R O U N D
B   R   W       U   M
A D J U S T   P A N A M A
G       S   R       R
  A T L A N T I C C I T Y
A   C   R   H   C       L
C H E A T   A R I Z O N A
I   O   N   V   N       N
D E C O R   D R E S S E D
```

Many S's (Page 84)

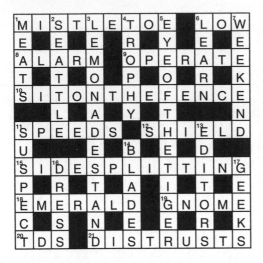

Trees and Slugs (Page 88)

Identical Chances (Page 86)

Toys and Games (Page 90)

Risky Thinking (Page 92)

A Globe-Spanning Career (Page 96)

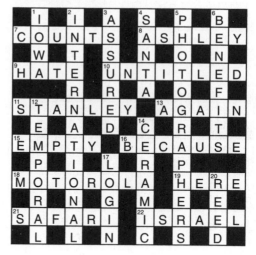

The High Life (Page 94)

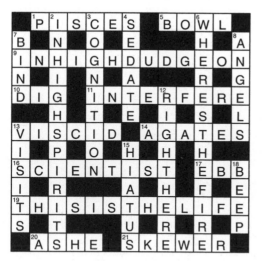

Miscellaneous (Page 98)

Paths and Perfection
(Page 100)

Mishmash (Page 104)

Stories and Characters
(Page 102)

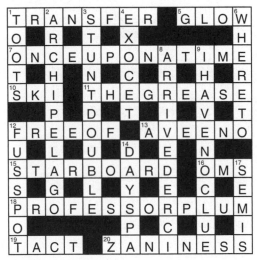

Phrases and Sayings
(Page 106)

A Sense of Place (Page 108)

Search and Find (Page 112)

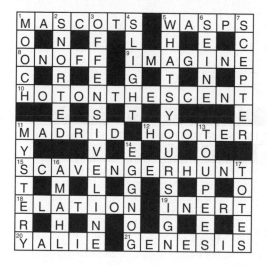

Books and Hobbies (Page 110)

Do You Know the Phrase? (Page 114)

Modern Life (Page 116)

Vintage Phrases (Page 120)

Grab Bag 2 (Page 118)

Common Expressions (Page 122)

Common Idioms (Page 124)

Food and Music (Page 128)

Mixed Bag (Page 126)

Potpourri (Page 130)

Assortment (Page 132)

What Did You Say? (Page 136)

Crossword Collection (Page 134)

Mishmash 2 (Page 138)

Random Knowledge (Page 140)

Music and Food (Page 144)

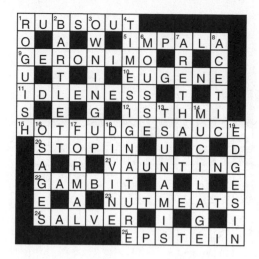

Arbitrarily (Page 142)

John Gotti (Page 146)

The Unabomber (Page 148)

Martin Scorsese Movies (Page 152)

Watergate (Page 150)

Making a Murderer (Page 154)

FBI Most Wanted (Page 156)

Chicago P.D. (Page 160)

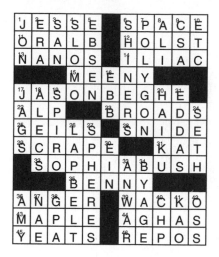

Famous Unsolved Crimes
(Page 158)

Charles Manson (Page 162)

Brooklyn Nine-Nine (Page 164)

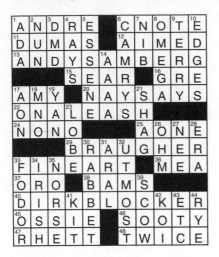

A	N	D	R	E		C	N	O	T	E
D	U	M	A	S		A	I	M	E	D
A	N	D	Y	S	A	M	B	E	R	G
			S	E	A	R		G	R	E
A	M	Y		N	A	Y	S	A	Y	S
O	N	A	L	E	A	S	H			
N	O	N	O			A	O	N	E	
		B	R	A	U	G	H	E	R	
F	I	N	E	A	R	T		M	E	A
O	R	O		B	A	M	S			
D	I	R	K	B	L	O	C	K	E	R
O	S	S	I	E		S	O	O	T	Y
R	H	E	T	T		T	W	I	C	E

Bernie Madoff (Page 168)

A	R	O	M	A		C	A	I	N	E
L	O	U	I	S		A	C	C	E	L
P	O	N	Z	I	S	C	H	E	M	E
E	S	C		S	A	T		B	E	V
S	T	E	F	A	N	I		E	S	E
			L	I	E		E	R	I	N
	M	R	E	D		A	V	G	S	
R	E	A	D		S	R	I			
E	S	T		P	U	R	L	I	E	U
A	S	A		A	L	I		K	A	N
L	I	F	E	S	A	V	I	N	G	S
M	A	I	L	S		A	D	E	L	E
S	H	A	M	E		L	O	W	E	R

Blue Bloods (Page 166)

M	O	I	S	T		C	A	P	T
I	N	T	W	O		H	I	R	E
S	E	E	I	T		I	M	I	N
T	O	M	S	E	L	L	E	C	K
		S	M	I	L	E	Y	S	
A	R	I		S	T	P			
L	A	D	S		E	I	G	H	T
A	M	Y	C	A	R	L	S	O	N
S	P	L	A	T		L	I	L	T
		M	L	B		X	E	S	
O	N	E	P	A	I	R			
V	A	N	E	S	S	A	R	A	Y
A	D	A	R		T	R	I	T	E
L	A	M	E		R	E	T	A	G
S	L	I	D		O	R	A	N	G

American Serial Killers (Page 170)

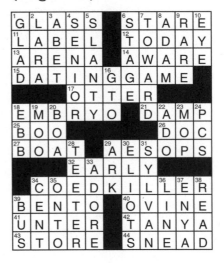

G	L	A	S	S		S	T	A	R	E
L	A	B	E	L		T	O	D	A	Y
A	R	E	N	A		A	W	A	R	E
D	A	T	I	N	G	G	A	M	E	
			O	T	T	E	R			
E	M	B	R	Y	O		D	A	M	P
B	O	O					D	O	C	
B	O	A	T		A	E	S	O	P	S
		E	A	R	L	Y				
	C	O	E	D	K	I	L	L	E	R
B	E	N	T	O		O	V	I	N	E
U	N	T	E	R		T	A	N	Y	A
S	T	O	R	E		S	N	E	A	D

192